Melton Mowbray

IN OLD PHOTOGRAPHS

Collected by TREVOR HICKMAN

An engraving of a drawing by John Throsby, originally published on 30 January 1790. This is possibly the earliest printed and published view of Melton Mowbray. Two farmers are shown approaching the town along what is now Scalford Road. One is riding a packhorse with panniers laden with Stilton cheese for sale at the weekly market in the town centre, held near the church of St Mary.

Melton Mowbray

IN OLD PHOTOGRAPHS

Alan Sutton Publishing Limited
Phoenix Mill · Far Thrupp · Stroud
Gloucestershire

First published 1993

By the same author:
Around Melton Mowbray in Old Photographs

British Library Cataloguing
in Publication Data

Hickman, Trevor
  Melton Mowbray in Old Photographs
  I. Title
  942.546

ISBN 0-7509-0430-5

Typeset in 9/10 Sabon.
Typesetting and origination by
Alan Sutton Publishing Limited.
Printed in Great Britain by
Redwood Books, Trowbridge.

Seal of John de Mowbray on a conveyance for a parcel of land purchased by Robert, son of Richard of Waltham, in December 1341. This land was located along the banks of the River Eye, near Brentingby.

Contents

Introduction

This book is a companion volume to *Around Melton Mowbray in Old Photographs*. It is not a history of the town but a selection of the old and not so old photographs that have been collected over a number of years by me and many of my friends, some of whom have helped with the book's preparation. Their names are recorded in the acknowledgements.

Melton Mowbray is a typical small Midlands market town, seemingly no different to other similar towns. It is only once you delve into the history of the area that you realize it is unique. Being a photographic collection, this history should commence in the late nineteenth century, but to add interest I have included photographs of prints, paintings and monuments that date back many centuries. The frontispiece is a detail of an eighteenth-century engraving showing two farmers approaching the town on the way to the local market just as farmers have done since before the Domesday Survey (1084–6), when the market that had been controlled by Geoffrey de Wirce since 1077 showed a return of twenty shillings per annum. Our market certainly dates from the Saxon period and has probably been held on a Tuesday for over a thousand years. The engraving shows St Mary's church standing high in the background as it has done since the thirteenth century. The artist illustrates a collection of thatched houses in the centre of the town, and on the extreme left stands a well built stone structure which could be The Limes built by Robert Hudson early in the 1600s and, like so many fine buildings in this town, demolished in this century in the name of progress.

Unfortunately that is the story of this market town: build, expand, destroy and build again. Could it have been any different? I doubt it. The town is a centre for trade and as such must cater to the demands of the merchants, the retailers and their customers. Fashions and the demand for locally produced goods change, so the town must change. The market has expanded over the centuries and, thankfully, it still does today. The fine fifteenth- and sixteenth-century houses built by merchants were all to be demolished. One of our finest local architects and builders, Christopher Staveley, *demolished* in 1780 the Mansion House that stood on the site of the present day St Mary's Way car park. Before the Mansion House was built the fortified Manor House of the Mowbrays, where King Richard Coeur de Lion stayed in 1194, stood in this area.

I have experienced considerable sadness looking at so many photographs of buildings that have been demolished in my lifetime, in some instances quite wantonly to my mind, but not of course to that of the town planners who must ensure that the prosperity of a thousand years continues. Growth is so important. This is a thriving market town, not a 'fossilized tourist centre relying on an interest in the past to generate income'. Historic buildings *can* blend in with modern interests, but not, I regret to say, in Melton Mowbray. It seems wrong and short sighted to me to have demolished the three Round Houses on Sage Cross Street, Woodville, the canal surveyor's house, and Thomas Moore's bakehouse on Thorpe End, and Elgin Lodge, that was John Ferneley's Studio. All these have gone since 1950 to be replaced with no substantial structure of modern architecture that could blend into the town of the future. What a tourist attraction these buildings would be now!

This then is a photographic record of much that has gone. I have included people wherever possible and have devoted one section to personalities in the town. For further reading on the history of this unique market town I suggest a browse through the pages of the following three books: *Melton Mowbray in Olden Times* by J. Ward (1879), *The Story of Melton Mowbray* by P.E. Hunt (1957), *Melton Mowbray, Queen of the Shires* by J. Brownlow (1980).

Having spent three years at school in the town, and worked at J.W. Warners at 2 South Parade for eleven years, all in the late 1940s and throughout the 1950s, I have witnessed many changes. At the time, as I have said, they were considered essential to the continuing prosperity of the town. My interest in the history of Melton Mowbray was generated by three people: John Greenslade, who appears on some of the 'official' photographs in this book; Norman Brooks, my works manager at Warners, who is standing in the centre of the group in the photograph on p. 126 (without Norman's interest none of the 1950s photographs of Chappie and Petfoods would have survived), and Jack Brownlow. In 1979 I helped Jack publish his marvellous book on Melton Mowbray; his knowledge of the history of the town was incredible.

From what we would now call a small village the town has grown into the urban community we inhabit today. A centre for the sale of agricultural products in the Saxon period, it became involved in the wool trade during the medieval period. With the sixteenth- and seventeenth-century enclosures the agriculture-based economy of the area changed and cheese made its appearance. The arrival of the canals in the late eighteenth century opened up the area at the same time as fox hunting as a spectacular rural sport arrived. The hunters of foxes were instrumental in widening the market for stilton cheese and pork pies and the manufacture of these products expanded during the nineteenth century and continues to do so today. The prosperity of the town was maintained by the mining and processing of iron ore in the early part of this century. The manufacture of pet foods by an internationally famous food processing company since the early 1950s has ensured the prosperity of the town continues.

This, then, is my collection. I take full responsibility for the presentation of the photographs and for the omissions. In one hundred and sixty pages it is impossible to provide a complete photographic history of such an interesting place.

Trevor Hickman, June 1993

The Town

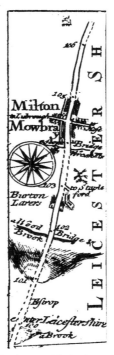

Melton Mowbray! Detail from the first published road atlas by Emanuel Bowen in 1720.

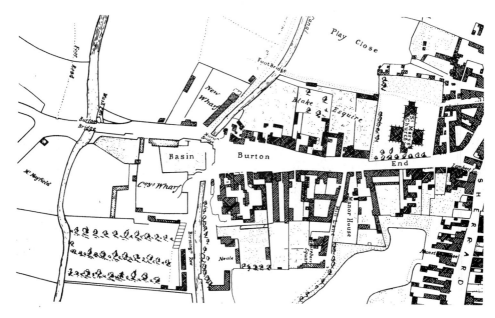

Plan of Burton Street (Burton End), *c.* 1840. This part of the town experienced considerable change with the building of the railway in the 1840s.

The canal bridge viewed from the New Wharf, looking into the Basin, *c.* 1870.

Burton Street Basin, the junction of the Melton Mowbray Navigation and the Oakham Canal, in the 1880s. The canal bridge shown in the photograph opposite is on the left, the Boat Inn is on the right.

The ford and stone bridge leading to the level crossing on Burton Street in 1890. A photograph of the crossing gates is on p. 22.

OAKHAM NAVIGATION.

RECEIVED the *31st* day of *March* 180*4* of Mr. *Richd Day Twentyfive* Pounds, being *Twentyfive* per Cent on *One* Shares in the intended Canal from MELTON MOW-BRAY to OAKHAM

29.
23.
24.th
25.
26.
Calls

£.   s.   d,

95 .. 0 .. 0 *Including*

£130 ..

Robt Hawley

Treasurer.

Clementson, Printer, Melton,

Interest — 3 – 14 – 5

A receipt for the final instalment on one share in the Melton to Oakham Canal Company, issued to Richard Day of Wymondham for share No. 183 after his death!

Burton Street in the great flood of 1908.

A horse being led to safety from one of the stables off Burton Street in the disastrous flood of 1899.

Burton Street 'Top End', showing Lamberts Lane, the narrow street that connected Burton Street with Sherrard Street before the First World War.

Spectators walking to Burton Races along Burton Street, *c.* 1900.

The Bede House Library and Museum in 1904. Originally built to house poor people of the town in 1646 as a result of a gift by Robert Hudson in 1638, the building was converted into a museum in 1847 by Mr W. Latham and Mr J. Woodcock.

Melton Carnival, 25 June 1925. This was the leading float on Burton Street, before it was conveyed around the town. The carnival queen Miss F. Caparn is seated in the centre. Left to right: Miss B. Rice, Miss Holmes, –?–, –?–, Miss P. Southerington, Miss M. Wallin, –?–. See p. 69.

Nurses from the War Memorial Hospital with a barrel organ collecting cash for the Melton Hospital fête, June 1936. They are outside the Bede Houses on Burton Street.

Burton Street, 1928.

Anne of Cleves House/the Old Rectory (now a restaurant), Burton Street in 1904.

A view of the town in 1911 showing the Burton Street bridge on the left.

Burton Street, 1904. The Colles Hall built in 1890 to the memory of the Revd W.M. Colles is on the left, while the Crown public house is on the right. The licensee was Henry Biddles.

A general view of Burton Street, c. 1928. Note the petrol pumps in front of the Melton Garage, built into the pavement.

Burton Street, *c.* 1950.

An advertisement dating from the 1940s.

Sutton Bros butchers, Burton Street, 1936.

The Melton Garage, Burton Street, 1936.

The Boat Inn and Toad Hall, Burton Street, 1965.

Birmingham Row off Burton Street, 1965. These houses were built for canal workers employed on the Melton and Oakham Navigations in around 1800, and were demolished in the 1970s.

The Midland Railway station, 1910.

The level crossing, Burton Street, 1895.

Sidings and storage area outside the Midland Railway station, 1967.

An extension to the sidings shown in the photograph above, and the junction with the main line.

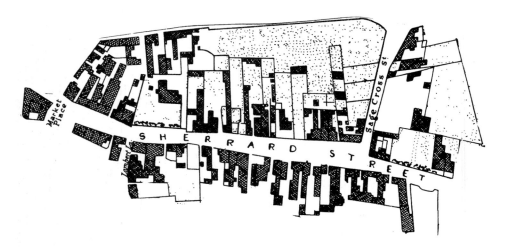

Sherrard Street, *c.* 1840.

Sherrard Street in the winter of 1880. The horse drawn cab stands opposite the entrance to Lamberts Lane.

The Marquis of Granby public house on Sherrard Street, 1910. Edward Cragg was the licensee. The Whitsuntide parade is passing by, being led by the town band, on its way to Thorpe End.

Sherrard Street, *c.* 1908. The tree on the left stands in the grounds of The Limes and is opposite Lamberts Lane, which leads to Burton Street. The photographer was standing in the Market Place.

Sherrard Street looking towards Thorpe End, 1916. The photographer stood opposite Lamberts Lane, and the boundary wall to The Limes is on the left.

A view of the Market Place, *c.* 1920. Lamberts Lane is on the left and has been widened. The trees in the grounds of The Limes had certainly become overgrown. It is hard to believe that Woolworths now stands on the site of this house.

The Black Swan ('Mucky Duck') public house (licensee George Robinson) on the right, with the Old Bishop Blaize public house (licensee John Thomas Smith) opposite, 1920. The entrance to Windsor Street is on the left.

A typical 1920s advertisement, printed on a paper bag.

EMILIE BULL

Millinery and Robes of Distinction

29 Sherrard Street, MELTON MOWBRAY

Albert Edward Grimbley, brush manufacturer, standing in the doorway to his shop, 10 Sherrard Street, 1916.

The street market on Sherrard Street in the 1920s. The Variety Stores stands on the corner of Windsor Street.

Belvoir Hunt leaving the Market Place, 1950. It is passing Sharman and Ladbury's garage.

Sherrard Street in the 1950s, looking towards the Market Place.

Part of Sharman and Ladbury's garage staff, 1948. Left to right: J. Stevens, M. Charles, W. Cheshire, H. Wright, G. Ames, H. Barratt. The photograph was taken at the rear of the garage in Elms Road.

Mr F.A. Payne and Miss I. Bodycote, Sales Manager and Secretary of Sharman and Ladbury, 1937.

Harpers Cycle Co. Ltd, 47 Sherrard Street, 1937. Six cycles are displayed on the pavement.

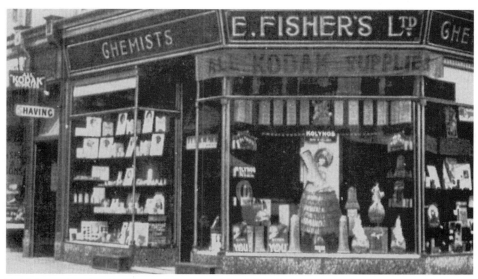

E. Fisher, chemist, 2 Sherrard Street, 1937. The shop was on the corner with Burton Street.

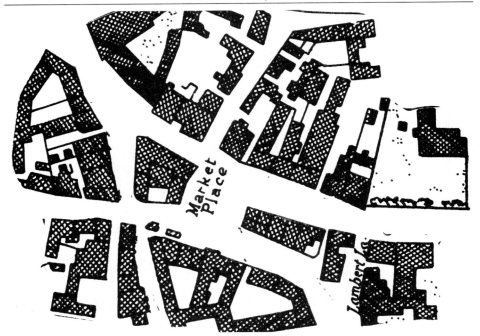

A plan of the Market Place in the middle of the nineteenth century, showing the surrounding streets and lanes.

The centre of Melton Mowbray, showing the Tuesday market, 1892. The photograph was taken from the battlements of St Mary's church.

Belvoir Hunt and hounds in the Market Place, 1936.

The Marquis of Waterford and his gang painting the White Swan red. Many historians consider that this is how the phrase 'painting the town red' originated. The incident was a result of consuming too much wine at the Croxton Park races on 6 April 1837.

Cheese Fair, 1904. In the background to the left is Towne & Co., stationer and printer, 28 Market Place. Harry Holmes was proprietor. In the centre stands Wing and Son, grocer and chemist, 29 Market Place – now the premises of W.H. Smith, stationer and bookseller.

The Market Place, 1908.

A halfpenny issued in Melton Mowbray in 1666 by Roger Waite, a local trader. The shortage of coins of the realm owing to the Civil War resulted in thousands of local trading tokens being issued throughout the country. This of course gave a monopoly of business to the person issuing the tokens, as his coin could only be spent in his own trading establishment.

Melton Mowbray is the centre for the marketing of Stilton cheese, which gets its name from the village of Stilton on the Great North Road in Northamptonshire. This old print was published on a cigarette card by Hignetts in 1925. Stilton probably originated in the dairy of Kirby Bellars manor house, the home of Sir Erasmus de la Fontaine, two miles to the south-west of Melton Mowbray, in the late seventeenth century. His daughter, Lady Belmont, passed the recipe on to the cook at Quenby Hall, Elizabeth Scarbrow, later Mrs Orton.

The Market Place, 1925. Left to right: William Barnes & Co., general and fancy draper, milliner, dress and mantle maker, outfitter and gentlemen's mercer, 20 Market Place; Pearks Stores, grocer; J. Towne & Co., stationer, printer, dealer in fancy goods and toys and circulating library.

Market Place viewed from Sherrard Street, with the 'Barnes block' centre background, 1920.

Melton Mowbray horse parade, 1910.

The Market Place laid out for the street party that celebrated the coronation of King George VI, 1937. Warners Café and fruiterers, 6 and 7 Market Place, is shown.

A 1940s advertisement for a café that was 'Mecca' for visiting villagers to the market town in the dark days of the Second World War.

A dramatic photograph taken at night of the Swan porch, 1967.

A view from the first floor window of W.H. Smith, looking into the market square, early 1950s.

W. E. Warner Limited

MARKET STORES

Melton Mowbray

R.A.C. RESTAURANT

PARTIES CATERED FOR

CONFECTIONERS

PORK PIE MANUFACTURERS

Telephone: 33 (Private Branch Exchange)

Telegrams: "KEENKUT" Melton

A 1940s advertisement for a splendid restaurant to the left of the photograph above, where the compiler of this collection spent many happy hours on market days in his youth. It is now the home of Thomas Cook, travel agent.

Barnes, Pearks, Towns and The Public Boot Benefit Company in 1916.

The Market Place, 1936.

Tuesday market, 1936.

Cheapside and South Parade viewed from the Market Place, c. 1969. The 'Barnes block' had been demolished by this time.

The famous Swan porch after the disastrous fire of 18 September 1985. The Grapes public house is on the right. Shortly after this photograph was taken the whole of the porch collapsed, but the blackened white swan was rescued and cleaned. In the cleaning process all the red paint daubed on by the Marquis of Waterford in 1837 was finally removed. The porch has been rebuilt but now stands on classical stone columns!

Belvoir Hunt accepting a stirrup cup from Warners Café in front of W.H. Smith, *c.* 1950.

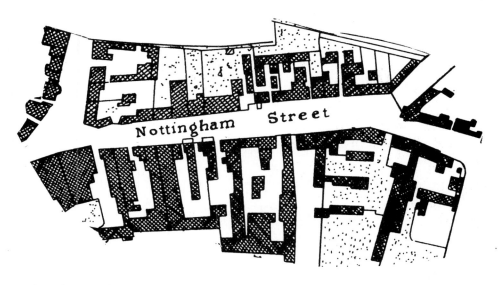

A plan of Nottingham Street in the middle of the nineteenth century.

The Baptist chapel with the White Lion Inn on the left in the 1890s.

Revd W.G. Anderson officiated at the Baptist chapel in Nottingham Street in 1934. He was a missionary in Africa from 1892 until 1900.

An 1890s advertisement for a famous hunting ale brewed in Whissendine, which was sold on Nottingham Street, Melton Mowbray.

The Bell Hotel on Nottingham Street, and looking towards Cheapside, South Parade and the Market Place, 1900. The crossroads at this point was Cornhill, and the lamppost occupies the site of the old Corn Cross.

Nottingham Street, 1904. The Eight Bells public house is on the right, where the licensee was William Wood.

The Old Kings Head (licensee Rice Cameron), 1920, before the extensive modernization programme.

Barclays Bank and the Bell Hotel, 1936.

E. Hollingshead, 27 and 28 Nottingham Street, saddler and manufacturer of hunting equipment, 1937.

W.H. Houghton & Co., 15 Nottingham Street, 1937. The shop was agent for BSA, Triumph, Norton, Sunbeam, OK Supreme and Royal Enfield motor cycles, pedal cycles and tandems.

Sharpe's Stores, hardware dealer, 10 and 11 Nottingham Street, 1937.

Sharpe's Stores delivery van on Scalford Road, *c.* 1930, loaded ready for a run in the local countryside. Sharpe's made a weekly delivery of paraffin and other essential commodities to outlying villages, hamlets, farms and houses.

A 'Bull Nose' Morris stands outside the Bell Hotel, where A.E. Wemyss was the proprietor, 1936. Boots the Chemist is on the left in South Parade. Leonard Gill, ironmongers, is situated in the 'Barnes block' in the middle distance.

Skinner and Rook, wine and spirit merchants, 37 Nottingham Street, 1937. The manager was T.R. Knight.

A pre-Second World War advertisement for one of Melton Mowbray's famous pork pie manufacturers.

The Corn Exchange, with Dickinson and Morris next door, 1936.

The Duke and Duchess of Gloucester attending the British Legion Ball at the Corn Exchange, 1936. They resided at Warwick Lodge during the hunting season.

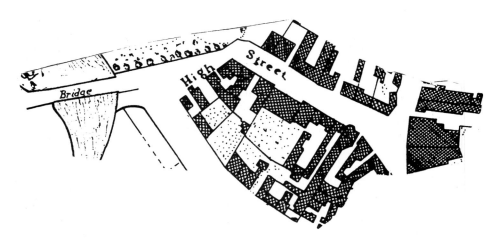

High Street in the nineteenth century, long before Wilton Road was built.

High Street, 1906. The photograph was taken by W. Till of 19 and 20 Burton Street, photographer and picture framer.

A painting by John Ferneley of Mr G. Petre's coach leaving the George Hotel on High Street, 1818.

The George Hotel, 1916. Henry William Sampey was the manager. In the centre background is the Bell Hotel, where Miss Mary Hammond was proprietress.

J. ATTENBURROW

M.P.S.   PHARMACIST

DISPENSING AND
        AGRICULTURAL CHEMIST

PERFUMES AND
            TOILET REQUISITES

1 HIGH STREET,
        MELTON MOWBRAY
            Telephone: 84

Advertisement for Attenburrow's chemist, with a photograph of the owner Mr James Attenburrow, 1937.

Photograph of Dr Montague Dixon MD and the White House, High Street, his home, 1902.

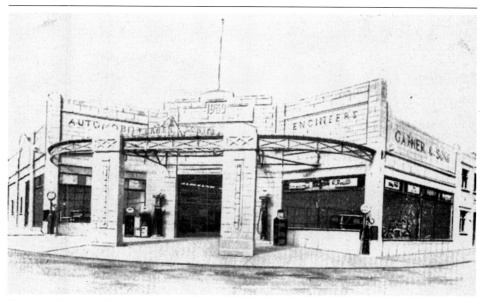

Garners Garage, 1936. It was on the corner of High Street and Wilton Road.

Mr G.H. Pidgeon and Mr J. Elliot, Sales Manager and Service Manager respectively, of Garner and Sons, 1937.

Plan of South Parade and Cheapside in the middle of the nineteenth century.

South Parade, leading to Nottingham Street, and Cheapside, leading to High Street, 1885. The thatched cottage in the centre background faced Corn Hill. It was demolished in 1897.

South Parade, 1890.

J.W. Warners, printer, bookbinder, publisher, bookseller, stationer and circulating library, 2 South Parade, 1904.

POST CARD.

This space may be used for Communication when for transmission in the British Isles.

THE ADDRESS ONLY TO BE WRITTEN HERE.

WINTER
BOOTS.

Be prepared for the coming severe winter (confidently prophesied by some weather experts) by purchasing your Winter Boots early.

Our Celebrated Strong Winter Boots are first and foremost in the field and are unequalled for Wear or Value.

HOLGATE'S
LEICESTER BOOT Co.,
3, South Parade,
Melton Mowbray.

Warner's Series.

Mr A H Marsh
Park Road
Melton Mowbray

Postcard forwarded to Mrs A.H. Marsh from the Holgate Boot Co. The card was printed by Warners of 2 South Parade and posted in 1908.

Tylers of 3 South Parade, 1937. They had taken over the premises of the Holgate Boot Co.

W. A. HEAP,

𝔚𝔦𝔫𝔢 & 𝔖𝔭𝔦𝔯𝔦𝔱 TRADE MARK. 𝔐𝔢𝔯𝔠𝔥𝔞𝔫𝔱,

MANUFACTURER OF THE CELEBRATED

PURE MINERAL WATERS AND LEMONADE,

PREPARED ONLY WITH FILTERED SPRING WATER,

KING STREET HOUSE AND CHEAPSIDE,

MELTON MOWBRAY.

Lemonade and Soda Water supplied in the Patent Syphon specially adapted for Invalids.

Advertisement published in the 1890s. William Albert Heap brewed beer on his premises in King Street, retailing it on Cheapside.

The Cheapside of the 'Barnes block', 1880s. Note the town pump in front of S. Manchester's, general furnisher.

W. Easom, grocer, commenced business in 1790 and traded through the reigns of eleven monarchs, closing down in the 1960s.

Garners on Cheapside, 1937. The shop was established in 1740.

Cheapside, looking towards South Parade, c. 1905.

W. Bowley and Co., proprietor W.E. Katz, jeweller, silversmith and optician on the corner of Cheapside in the 'Barnes block', 1936.

Brownlow, chemist and druggist, 6 Cheapside, 1936.

Cheapside on the right, South Parade on the left, and the 'Barnes block' in the centre, 1936.

Three Tuns public house, 3 King Street, 1912. John Meadows was the publican.

M. Bull, farrier for fox hunters, in his forge off King Street, 1911.

Jacob Brotherhood's travelling horse drawn van in 1916. His shop was at 53 and 54 King Street.

The Plaza cinema, King Street. Built in 1918, it was converted to a bingo hall in the 1950s, and demolished in July 1982 as part of a road improvement scheme.

Two horse drawn vans loaded ready for trading in the surrounding villages. Picks Stores was situated at 1 Kings Road.

Aerial view of Kings Road, 1933, showing the Midland Woodworking Company and the Snow Hill brick pits.

The Golden Fleece public house, 1891. John Simpson was publican.

C.B. Payne's furniture shop on the corner of Park Lane, 1 Leicester Street, 1905.

The grocer's shop of Miss Mary Ann Allen, 1898, standing on the corner of Timber Hill and Sage Cross Street. It was adjacent to the imposing structure of the Wesleyan chapel, where the ministers were the Revd Robert Daw and the Revd Ralph Calderbank.

The Round Houses, Sage Cross Street, built in the grounds of The Limes towards the end of the eighteenth cuntury at the expense of the Stokes family, and occupied by three maiden sisters. The houses, octagonal in shape, contained three rooms, and the gardens where the same size as each house. They were unique, and when this photograph was taken in 1911 they were considered to be of considerable architectural importance. The houses were wantonly demolished in 1980 to make way for a doctor's surgery.

The tollgate that stood at the junction of Thorpe Road and Saxby Road on Thorpe End in 1837, when the Marquis of Waterford with his unruly crew painted the gates and the keeper's cottage red. See p. 33.

Thorpe End viewed from Sherrard Street, 1904. The Marquis of Granby public house is on the right; Edward Cragg was publican. Thomas Moore's bakehouse, 1 Thorpe End, stands centre left. It has been long since demolished in a road widening scheme.

Carnegie Library on Thorpe End, photographed shortly after it was opened in 1904. Mr Andrew Carnegie donated £2,000 towards the construction of the building on land donated by the town estate. It is now the tourist centre and museum.

The start of the Melton Carnival parade outside the Carnegie Library, 25 June 1925.

The Wheatsheaf public house, Thorpe End, demolished as part of a road improvement scheme on 28 December 1983.

Thorpe Road, 1904. On the right is the entrance to Stafford Avenue. Thorpe Road post office stands on the corner. John Thomas Bilson was the post office clerk.

Leicester Road bridge, 1903.

Leicester Road, 1905. Egerton Park is on the left, open fields on the right. These are now the Town Estate recreation park and tennis courts.

Carson's Garage, owned by Mr Peter Weaver, 1936.

St Mary's church morning Sunday School class, 1934, with Miss Margaret Sansby.

The junction of Nottingham Road, Asfordby Road and Park Road, now Norman Way. See also p. 77.

Nottingham Road, 1918. The entrance to the Crescent is on the left of the photograph.

A painting by Claude Ferneley of his father, John, working in his studio at Elgin Lodge, Scalford Road, *c.* 1825.

A Class B1 in full steam leaving the Melton Northern station bound for Skegness, *c.* 1940. The cantilever signal box on the left of the photograph was to a London & North Western Railway design, and swayed in high winds!

Entrance to the refreshment rooms and toilets on the Northern station, *c.* 1950.

The entrance to the refreshment room when the railway station on Scalford Road was being demolished, 1967. A fine example of terracotta work was lost forever.

The last days of a magnificent railway station, 1967.

London & North Eastern Railway bridge crossing Scalford Road, 1969.

Entrance to Quorn Avenue on Asfordby Road, 1930.

Traffic island on the Asfordby Road, Nottingham Road, Park Road and Wilton Road junction, *c.* 1950.

Shouler's saleroom on Norman Street, demolished in the building of the relief road Norman Way in the 1980s.

The last day. Miss Cicely Maycock, headmistress (with basket), saying goodbye to all her children on the day that St Mary's Norman Street Church of England Infants School closed for the last time, 1 July 1977.

Entrance to the War Memorial Hospital on Ankle Hill, 1928. The memorial to the left of the gateway has been removed since this photograph was taken.

Dalby Road near the junction with Leicester Road, 1926. The swimming baths now occupy the overgrown area to the right of the photograph.

Dalby Road, looking down the hill, *c.* 1905. Ankle Hill is to the right of the photograph.

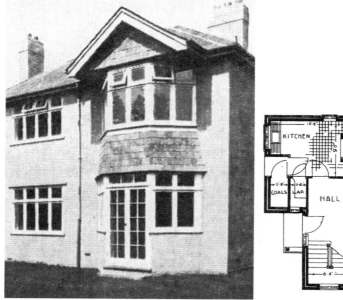
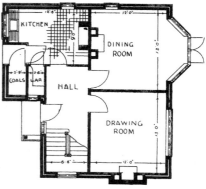

Green Acre, The Drive, Dalby Road, built by E. Clarke and Sons for Mr W. Bailes in the early 1930s for £850. This is one of the quality houses built by Clarkes in Melton Mowbray on the Dalby Road estate before the Second World War.

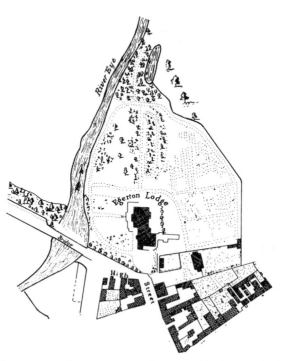

SECTION TWO
Stately Residences

Plan of Egerton Lodge, *c.* 1840. Wilton Road had yet to be built.

Egerton Lodge, 1903, before the extensive demolition of part of this historic house.

Mr Arthur Vickris Pryor DL, JP, who resided at Egerton Lodge when the photograph above was taken. Mr Pryor was educated at Eton, was a Justice of the Peace, and hunted with the Quorn, Belvoir and Cottesmore hounds; he was Deputy Lieutenant for Leicestershire and married Elizabeth Countess of Wilton, the owner of Egerton Lodge, in 1886. See p. 153.

Melton Mowbray Urban District Council, photographed at the grand opening of Melton Mowbray Town Hall, Egerton Lodge, on 10 October 1929. Front row, left to right: J. Sparling, H.C. Holmes, T. Brown, R.W. Brownlow, W. Greaves, O. Brotherhood, G.H. Hinman. Back row: E. Steans, C.S. Jenkins, G.W. Goodacre, W.H. Jarvis (surveyor and engineer), H.K. Barker (clerk), E.D. Hayes, F.R. Bailey, G.W. Selby.

The Town Hall and Gardens, Egerton Lodge, 1936.

Woodville, a charming house, 65 Burton Street, 1962. This was built in 1837 for Joseph Neale, surveyor to the Oakham Canal Company navigation system.

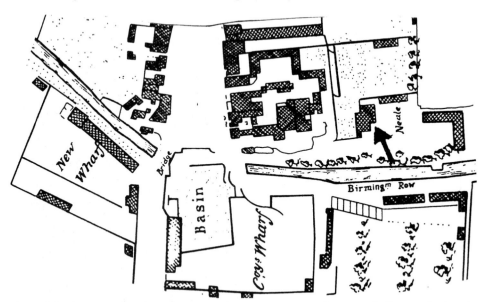

Plan of the basin and surrounding area drawn two years after Woodville was built. The house is indicated with an arrow. The bay window on the left was added later. An important building, part of our industrial heritage, it was demolished by Pedigree Petfoods in the early 1980s.

Newport Lodge was built in 1849. The Earl of Bradford made extensive alterations, converting the house to a fine hunting lodge. It is seen here in 1903.

Captain Robert Bunten Muir in residence at Newport Lodge, 1903. He held the rank of Major in the Leicestershire Yeomanry and was Captain of the 65th Squadron, 17th Battalion in the Boer War for thirteen months. Captain Muir hunted with all three local packs of hounds.

The Limes, 1903. It is hard to imagine that the shops in the centre of Melton Mowbray now occupy the site of this splendid house. A tragic loss of an historic and architecturally important building.

Mr James Pacey JP, the owner of The Limes when the photograph above was taken. He purchased the property in 1889 for £3,000. Mr Pacey was born at Garthorpe in 1846 and at the time this photograph was taken in 1903 was a partner in the local brewery, Adcock, Pacey and Company, brewers of fine beer.

Hamilton Lodge was built in 1902 by Gavin, 2nd Lord Hamilton of Dalzell, KCVO. Frances, Countess of Warwick purchased the house a few years later and renamed it Warwick Lodge. The Duke and Duchess of Gloucester rented the property in 1935 for a number of seasons. In 1955 the house was purchased by the Melton and Belvoir Rural District Council for use as their offices and council chambers.

Melton and Belvoir RDC, at Warwick Lodge, May 1961. Back row, left to right: D. Headly, Revd R.T. Seivewright, A. Livingstone, E.W. Green, S.W. Birch, H.E. Hickling, R.W. Toon, G. Abbott, D.F. Sanday, S.S. Exton, L.E. Jesson. Centre row, left to right: H.L. Brown, G.E. Dalton, F.T. Whait, W.R. Allwood, H. Lord, S.W. Warrington, W. Miller, H.D. Hornsby, H. Smith, S.A. Eggleston, P.F. Dalton, L. Thacker, G.M. Hutchinson, J.K. Hart, G.H. Houghton, D. Babbington-Smith. Front row, left to right: T. Thurman, Mrs P.E. Garratt, Mrs M.B. Lee, W.E. Stanley, J.G. Burgin, A.P. Marsh (clerk), P.R. Hill (chairman), J.F. Groome (vice chairman), W.T. Orson, Mrs M.L. Aspell, Mrs L.R. Croome, H.A. Lewis (treasurer), J.P. Milburn (surveyor).

Colonel Charles Wyndham purchased Hill House on Ankle Hill in the early 1840s, then proceeded to build a house, seen here in 1906, that he named Wyndham Lodge. Colonel Wyndham had an exciting army career, serving with the Scots Greys in the Peninsular War, and fighting with Wellington at Waterloo.

War Memorial Hospital, Melton Mowbray, Wyndham Lodge. In August 1920 Colonel Richard Dalgleish agreed to purchase Wyndham Lodge and 15 acres of land for converting to a hospital for £5,000 and also pay for the necessary alterations amounting to £2,000. The property was to be used as a cottage hospital in perpetuity in memory of the local lads who had died in the First World War. It was opened on 19 January 1922. See p. 79.

This house, seen here in 1912, was built in 1870 by Mr Thomas Hickson at a cost of £2,986 10s, and was named Staveley Lodge after Christopher Staveley, the local architect who designed many fine buildings in Melton Mowbray. During the Second World War it was the headquarters of a Parachute Brigade who dropped behind enemy lines at Arnhem. After the war it became the main offices for the Production Engineering Research Association (PERA).

The laboratories, workshops and offices of PERA at Staveley Lodge being overshadowed by a crane, during the construction of the Melton Mowbray Borough Council Offices on Nottingham Road.

Craven Lodge, seen here *c.* 1910, was built in 1827 by Dr Keal and called Burton House. It was purchased in 1856 by the Hon. W.G. Craven, who made extensive alterations and re-named the house.

In 1922 Craven Lodge was purchased by Captain Michael Wardell, who divided the house into several fine apartments to be let to the hunting fraternity. In 1923 the Prince of Wales took one of the apartments, and this photograph taken in 1925 shows the wing of the house that he occupied.

The Prince of Wales was a frequent visitor to Craven Lodge from 1923 to 1929, and hunted with all the local packs of hounds. This photograph taken in 1935 shows the Prince at the races with Mrs Simpson, whom he first met at Burrough Court, Burrough-on-the-Hill, a few miles to the south-east of Melton Mowbray.

In 1793 this property was called Norman House. Later it became The House, and when this photograph was taken in 1903 it was called The Elms, so named by Lieutenant Colonel William Thomas Markham who purchased the property in 1867. The house was acquired by Dr and Mrs Lionel Powell in 1893. On the death of Dr Powell in 1930 the house became derelict, and was pulled down.

The Second World War intervened and the site of The Elms was a vacant lot containing rubble and crumbling walls for many years. In 1958 a modern telephone exchange was constructed here, finally replacing the ornamental garden and magnificent house that stood for over 150 years in the centre of Melton Mowbray.

SECTION THREE

Industry and Commerce

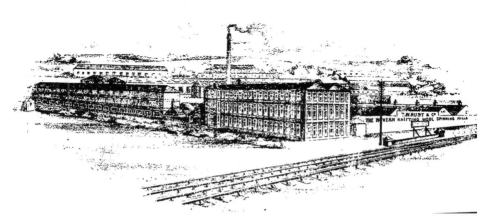

A late nineteenth-century factory, T.W. Rust and Company's Spinning Mill. It was on the site of Pedigree Petfoods food processing plant.

Enoch Evans with some of his employees standing outside his factory on Thorpe End. This photograph was taken in the 1890s. Messrs Evans and Co. was the first factory to manufacture commercially large quantities of pork pies, commencing in 1830.

An advertisement for Evans's hand raised pork pies, 1940s. Note the telephone number 5: no problems with six figure STD numbers when that telephone was installed!

Flo Stevens and helpers pour the liquid jelly into Melton Mowbray pork pies.

John Crosher shows John Greenslade and a party of schoolboys how Stilton cheese is made, 1947.

An advertisement, 1940s. Stilton cheese could only be produced under licence as it was considered a luxury, which was not necessary to sustain the war effort.

Eddy Fryer tips the local farmers' milk into the weigh bowl.

Harry Searle operates the milk pasteurizer.

Linda Hammond pierces Stilton cheese to enable the famous blue mould to form.

Jim Mayfield, head cheesemaker, on the left of the photograph, assists in cutting the Leicester cheese curd.

E. Clarke and Sons and the Midlands Woodworking Co. on Kings Road, Melton Mowbray shared a number of facilities on the factory site during their early years. This photograph of 1925 shows the first three ladies to be employed in the combined works at the entrance to the shared office. Standing, left to right: Miss Ena Goodacre, Miss Janet Marchent (the first lady employees of the Midland Wordworking Co.). Seated: Miss Olive Rowell (the first lady to be employed by E. Clarke and Sons).

Midland Woodworking lorry standing outside Snow Hill Garage, *c*. 1935. The garage was a subsidiary of the Midland Woodworking Co.

Outside Snow Hill Garage, 1933. Left to right: Fred Terry, Vic Bennett, –?–, Fred Gaunt, E. Glitheroe.

Edward Portess in front of Snow Hill Garage with his dog Spot, 1947.

One of the many joint projects that were entered into between E. Clarke and Sons and the Midland Woodworking Co. was constructing the horse operating theatre for the Royal Army Veterinary Corps, Welby Lane, Melton Mowbray. Left to right: Gordon Hart, Phillip Chittenden.

Printing the *Times* on the hand fed Wharfedale Press, 1911.

Mr J. Meadows working the linotype machine, 1936.

Setting type by hand in the composing room, 1936. The head of the department, Mr J. Burman, 'standing at his case', is on the left.

The first days! Don Harrison and his team tearing down part of the Paton and Baldwin factory in April 1951, before Chappie Ltd set up business.

The first retort arrives at Melton Mowbray, 1951. Chappie Ltd starts production.

The first load of petfood being dispatched from Chappie Ltd, 1952.

Chappie apprentices, March 1955. Left to right: P. Taft, R. Dyckhoff, A. Lawson, J. Gaunt (head of training), M. Yapp, W. Sawicki, J. French.

The first poster issued by Chappie Ltd, to be posted on hoardings on selected sites around the country in May 1955. The company also considered going into films at this time, featuring Miss Kit-E-Kat and her family, as part of their advertising programme.

Ron Acton, a member of the Red Shift maintenance crew, working his lathe, May 1955.

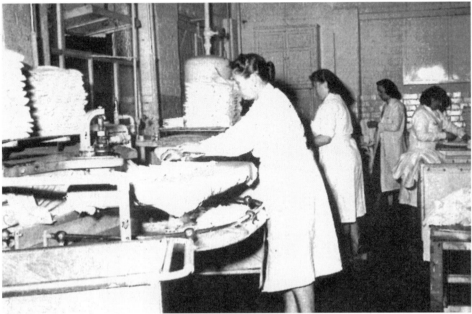

Chappie Ltd laundry, July 1955. It processed 16,000 garments per week. The manager of this unit was Mr E.W. Langford.

Bridging the Scalford brook, September 1955.

A few months later. The new bridge serving the factory exit in 1956.

The first traffic lights to be permanently erected in Melton Mowbray, November 1955. They were to control the flow of traffic from Chappie Ltd on to Mill Street.

The four catering supervisors, November 1957. Left to right: Miss K. Doyle, Mrs D. Hyde, Mrs A. Wildon, Mrs G. Degg.

Mrs Phyllis Miller (née Welbourn) of Wymondham distributing light refreshments in the canteen, July 1955. Mrs Miller was born in Wymondham in 1918, served in the RAF during the Second World War as an administrative NCO, and joined Chappie Ltd in 1953.

Factory scenes, 1955. Top left: Arthur Hubbard filling the retorts using an overhead gantry. Top right: Mr K. Polec unloading tins in the goods-in department. The conveyor in the foreground delivered the cans to the filling station. Bottom left: Dennis Atkinson driving his 'stacatruc'. Bottom right: a new innovation for the food preparation department in 1955 was the installation of a Wetter bandsaw for cutting up frozen blocks of meat. Mr John Paszynski is seen operating it.

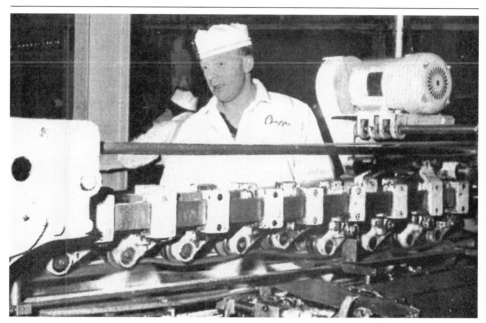

Ron Hurd working the labelling machine, January 1956. Ron worked for Paton and Baldwin, and was one of the first people to join Chappie Ltd when they took over the site in 1951.

Roof maintenance by the permanent maintenance team, July 1956. Left to right: Reg Marshall, Gordon Hack, George Davie.

A battery of retorts in full steam, 1956.

Jack Bonser operating a can
unscrambler in September
1956. Jack, a keen local
cricketer, played for Egerton
Park, averaging thirty-two runs
per innings during the 1954
season.

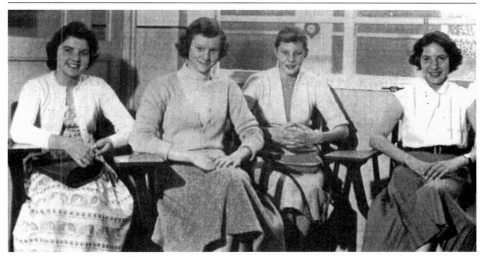

New recruits to the office training scheme, September 1956. Left to right: Miss Anne Payne, Miss Pamela Hopkins, Miss Jane Ball, Miss Joan Lester.

Mr G. Southerington maintaining a steady head of steam in the boiler room, April 1957. Mr Southerington served in the Royal Artillery Signals Division during the Second World War. He took part in the Battle of Arnhem, being taken prisoner after eight days of fighting.

Sheep pens in the cattle market off Scalford Road, 1950.

Fatstock pens, 1968, the year in which the grand re-opening by the Rt. Hon. Cledwyn Hughes MP took place.

SECTION FOUR

Education,
Recreation and
Pastimes

An engraving of St. Mary's Church in 1879 by Claude Ferneley.

Children in the Play Close, 1902.

Sheep grazing in the Play Close, 1904.

The Play Close, *c*. 1910.

The entrance to the Play Close and Town Park on Leicester Street was improved by the Town Estate in 1907 and 1909, when the town wardens were Henry Wood and R.W. Brownlow.

Children's bathing pool in the Play Close, 1936. This popular pool has long since been removed, in the cause of good hygiene.

Ladies relaxing on the grass in front of the bandstand in the park, *c.* 1925.

The 'landing stage' and steps down to the River Eye just before the First World War, when rowing on the river was a pleasant Sunday afternoon pastime.

Rowing on the River Eye to the west of Egerton Park, *c.* 1910.

Two moored rowing boats and a dinghy in full sail on the River Wreake near Sysonby church, before the First World War.

The 'duck raft' in front of Egerton Lodge when it was still the Council Offices. These rafts were maintained at the expense of the Borough Council.

The street party on Nottingham Street to celebrate Queen Elizabeth II's Silver Jubilee, 7 June 1977.

A decorated lorry, part of Queen Elizabeth II's Silver Jubilee celebrations, leaving Thorpe End for Sherrard Street, 7 June 1977. It is Passing Parke House Garage with the Wesleyan chapel high in the background. Both these buildings have now been demolished.

Melton Rovers in Beeby's Yard off Burton Street, 1918–19 season. On the end of the second row, right, sits Gildene Sleath, with Jack Hazelwood sitting on the extreme left of the front row.

Representative side from Melton Mowbray and district schools, 1928–9 season. Back row, left to right: John Moore, Len Harker, Frank Harding, Walter Harris, John Bilby, Dagger Ward. Front row: Jack Williams, George Parr, John Bateson, Arthur Core, Cecil Muse.

The top class football team of the 1944–5 season that represented the RAF at Melton Mowbray. Back row, left to right: Andy Bromley, Bill Maclean, –?–, Flight Lieutenant Ames. Centre row: –?–, Alan Brown, Ted Sale, –?–, McKie, Oswald Destine, Roy Bentley. Front row: Clem Stevenson, Jimmy Learmonth, Fred Moon, Group Captain Gomez, Bert Brocklehurst, Fred Butcher, Jack Smith. Bill Maclean was the trainer for Leicester City Football Club before and after the Second World War.

Melton Town Football Club, 1948–9 season. Back row, left to right: George Calwell, Joe Eglestone, Dixie McNeil, Jack Rodgers, Arthur Core, Fred Parr. Front row: Haden Hicks, Jimmy Learmonth, Les Staff, Billy Caithness, Vic Orridge.

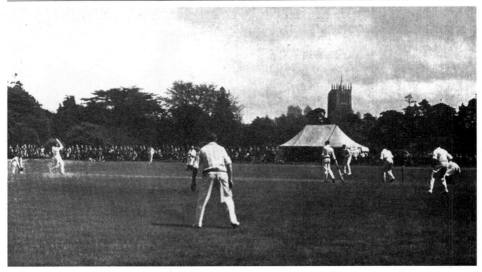

Leicestershire playing Somerset at Egerton Park, Melton Mowbray in the summer of 1946.

PLAYER'S CIGARETTES

Eddie Dawson of Sycamore House, Wymondham, 1934. He captained Leicestershire for four seasons between 1928 and 1933, and played for England in South Africa. Dawson was considered to be one of the finest batsmen who played for Cambridge before the Second World War.

Thorpe Arnold Cricket Club, 1931. Back row, left to right: I. Brown, S. Elsom, W. Smith, O. Lockton, H. Parkes, W. Hodgkinson. Front row: N. Tyrell, G. Fleckney, F. Hodgkinson, L. Perkins, S. Wyles.

Brian Keightley and Dennis Parr going out to bat on the Thorpe Arnold cricket ground, Thorpe Road, Melton Mowbray, 1965. Mrs Pearson and Michael are in the background.

Melton Town Ladies' Bowling Club, 1952, in front of the pavilion off Saxby Road. Standing on the steps of the pavilion, left to right: Mrs M. Portess, Miss E. Sharpe. Standing: Mrs Baxter, –?–, Mrs Fitzgerald, –?–, Mrs Sansby, Edith Plumb, Mrs Irons, Mrs Lister, Mrs Bisel, Eadie Payne, Anne Hibbert. Seated: Ester Barry, Mrs Plumb, Mrs Barton, Mrs Whitbread, Mrs Wormleighton, Mrs Chapman, Mrs Mee. Seated on the grass: Hilary Portess, Pamela Clamp.

Melton Town Gentlemen's Bowling Club, 1951. Standing, left to right: H. Cliff, C. Wesson, P. Lisle, –?–, C. Skinner, N. Brooks, C. Mayo, J. Barton, C. Pick, G. Payne, J. Williams, R. Arnold. Seated: E. Fitzgerald, R. Watts, H. Smith, P. Challis.

The observation post for the war-time observer corps was situated in a field behind Melbray Drive, off Scalford Road. Back row, left to right: Jack Brydges, ? Tuneley, Tom Golling, Hedley Clift, Ernie Bartram, Sid Saul, Frank Saunders, Stan Leach. Middle row: Ted ?, Steve North, Joe Morrison, Jack Golling, Charlie Walkden, Claude Hill. Front row: Rex Polendine, Bernard Turner, ? Lunn, Gordon Astill, Jess Tinkler, Tom Barnard.

Jess Tinkler, motor engineer and part-time observer in the Second World War. Before the D-Day landings Jess Tinkler, Rex Polendine and Joe Morrison were recruited as volunteers to assist in the landings on the Normandy beaches. This was a highly secretive mission. Business associates, family and friends did not know that these three were at sea on a variety of ships, acting as observers for the invading allied forces. This was particularly awkward for Jeff who was employed in a local garage. Rex and Joe were full-time observers, but Jess's absence as head of the service department for three months without any communication alienated his employers, who sacked him in his absence. On returning home this brave man found he had no job to go to. A fine thank you! Eventually he set up his own garage in Mill Street.

Wesleyan Band, *c.* 1920.

Melton Town Silver Prize Band, 1937. The conductor was Mr H.V. Dyson. Back row, left to right: Frank Hurd, Cyril Walker, Bill Guilford, John Way, Frank Handley, Vic Richardson, Charles Biddles, –?–, Sid Wesson. Middle row: Arthur Sisson, Arthur Bartram, Bill Hart, Arthur Slater, Harry Chatwin, Horace Handley, John Crowther, Sam Manchester, Randall Pollard, Bert Rands, Bert Page. Front row: Nobby Clarke, Charles Robinson, Frank Pollard, Whitley Brownlow, W.V. Dyson, Alfred Handley, Bill Wesson, Jack Pollard, Jack Kilby.

Melton Mowbray Operatic Society, 1930. Miss Anne Kestin and Aldith Roper in *Zurika*.

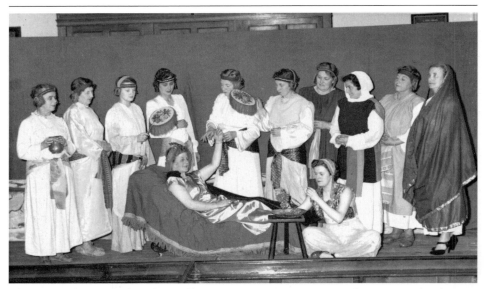

The Congregational chapel travelling concert party, *c.* 1950. This group of volunteer entertainers travelled around the villages in the Melton Mowbray area entertaining the locals in village halls and chapels.

The 'Tally Ho' band marching out of Nottingham Street into South Parade and Cheapside during the celebrations for Queen Elizabeth II's Silver Jubilee.

Melton Mowbray Cycle Club Committee, 1905. The founder of this club, Mr Harry Wesson, is seated in the front row on the left, in the light coloured jacket.

Harry and Lucy Wesson seated on the Hilda Cycle, named after their first daughter. Harry Wesson invented the Hilda Cycle, and traded from 5 Sage Cross Street. The photograph was taken on the Leicester Road, outside Egerton Park, in 1905.

The County Technical College, King Street, when it was opened in September 1937. This college was built on the site of the County Police Station built in 1842.

The first principal of the County Technical College, William Wall BSc, AIC.

The Old Police Station, King Street, built on the site of the Bridewell (prison). The Marquis of Waterford and some of his cronies spent a night in the Bridewell in April 1837, and did not think much of it!

Melton Mowbray Central Boys School, Limes Avenue, built in 1928.

HRH The Duke of Gloucester, who
officially opened the Central Boys
School on 7 December 1933.

Melton Mowbray Central Boys School, 1935. It is now the Brownlow Infants School.

Teaching staff of the Central Boys School surrounded by their pupils in 1933. Staff, left to right: L. Cullen, –?–, C. Walkden, L. Till, C. Goldspink, (Nunc) Hubbard, Holt, Peabody, C. Mayo, S. (Pop) Berry.

Melton Mowbray Modern Boys School prefects, 1948. Back row, left to right: Hendey, Exton, Hickman. Front row: Hebb, McNeill, Timbrell, Henfrey, Bonser.

The Coronation Party at Kings Road Infants School, 1953.

Kitchen staff of Kings Road Infants School, 1950. Left to right: Mabel Watkin, Mrs Startin, Mrs Dalby, –?–, Mrs Isherwood.

Kings Road Infants School staff, 1924. Back row, left to right: Miss Needham, –?–, Miss Branston, Miss Cox. Front row: Miss Cox, Mrs Brown (headmistress), Miss White, –?–.

Kings Road Infants School staff, 1940. Back row, left to right: Miss Branston, Miss Cox, Mrs Jenner. Front row: Elspeth ?, Miss White, Miss Needham (headmistress), Miss Wright, ?.

King Edward VII Grammar School, Burton Road, 1933.

Miss Mawby's class at King Edward VII Grammar School, 1952. Doug Ecob is holding an ice-cream cone over the head of Miss Mawby. Also in the group are: Davina Muggleton, Pat Lightfoot, Ann Jallands, Nora Wartnaby, Janet Lunn, Jackie Ray, Jill Wallace, Rosemary Hodgson, Wendy Cartwright, Pauline Shepherd, Pam Chaplin, Brigid Newbold, Ann Breward, Joy Middleton, Gwen Starbuck, Wendy Golling, Maureen Rippon, Marjorie Crawford, Janet Ash, David Foster, Cliff Baguley, Graham Brooks, Peter Lewis, Bruce Needham, Carl Wright, Mike Smedley, Oscar Lay, Gus Hewson, Geoff Wade, Jon Simson, Ron Bailey, Mike Thompson, Tony Hinman, John Wright and Brian Burt.

R. Stuart Smith BA, 1937. He was appointed headmaster of King Edward VII Grammar School in September 1911.

The Modern School for Girls in Wilton Road, opened by HRH The Duke of Gloucester in December 1933. It is now the County Library.

Miss N.E. Renno, headmistress of the Girls' Modern School, 1936.

Miss C. Packer MA, senior mistress in charge of girls at the King Edward VII Grammar School, 1937.

Miss M. Smith, headmistress of Melton Primary Girls School, 1936.

Miss E. Burnett, principal of the Cairn Holt School, Asfordby Road, 1936.

The Sarson Secondary School for Girls, Burton Road, *c.* 1960. This school replaced the girls' school on Wilton Road.

Melton Working Men's Club, 1937. Back row, left to right: P. Handley, H. Dobney, E. Richardson, K. Hart, F. Gillett, E. Hopkins. Front row: A. Wilmott, W. Bishop, H. Richardson, J. Spiby, G. Gresham.

Melton Branch of the British Legion, 1937. Back row, left to right: C. Cobley, E. White, W. Dawson, A. Bodsworth, T. Fletcher, E. Heawood, M. Newham. Middle row: S.N. Jones, W. Wade, R. Peters, Major-General J. Vaughan, T. Brooks, A. Blakemore, B. Pacey. Front row: A. Rowden, H. Rands.

Jack Skinner, May 1956. Local entertainer and part-time trick cyclist, he appeared on television during the late 1940s and early 1950s.

Personalities

Wood engraving of Anne of Cleves House, in front of St Mary's church, 1879.

The effigy of King Richard I in the Abbey church at Fontevrault. Richard Coeur de Lion visited Melton Mowbray in 1194, staying at the fortified manor house of William de Mowbray that stood on the site of St Mary's Way car park, near the Regal cinema. King Street was named after this king.

Effigy of King John. This unpopular king visited Melton Mowbray in 1208, 1209 and 1215, staying a number of days on each visit, principally to collect taxes and subdue his rebel barons – one of whom was William de Mowbray.

Richard III, who visited Melton
Mowbray on 25 September 1484, on his
way from Nottingham to Oakham.

Anne of Cleves. In 1540 King Henry VIII
gave part of the manor of Melton Mowbray
and a house that had belonged to the Melton
Priory to Anne of Cleves, on the
understanding that she retired to the country,
taking no part in court life. This she wisely
did. It is presumed she lived in Anne of
Cleves House on Burton Street. She led a
secretive life after the king had divorced her,
retaining her wealth, and her head.

145

HRH The Prince of Wales, later King Edward VII. This sporting prince enjoyed the good life in Melton Mowbray, maintaining a string of hunters in the town. When Stapleford Hall was put up for sale after the death of Lady Harborough, the royal prince endeavoured to purchase the estate. His mother thought it was too close to his Melton cronies and insisted that Sandringham was purchased instead. In May 1862 Sandringham became the prince's official residence, well away from Melton Mowbray. In the 1890s the east coast railway line was built, with a station at Sandringham, so the royal train had easy access to the 'flesh pots' of Melton Mowbray. See p. 94 in *Around Melton Mowbray in Old Photographs*.

John Ferneley. This famous sporting painter was born at Thrussington in 1782. Ferneley purchased some land on Scalford Road in 1813, first building a studio big enough to hold a horse. See p. 74. He then built Elgin Lodge as his home, so named after the Elgin Marbles in the British Museum. For nearly fifty years he lived in this house painting some of the finest hunting pictures ever produced. His house and studio was open to allcomers, and was visited by the young bloods of the town, princes and kings. On market days in the 1840s and '50s a stroll up to Ferneley's for a glass of port was the order of the day. He died in 1860 aged 78, and was buried in Thrussington churchyard.

A painting inside St Mary's church, dating from *c.* 1828. On the front left is John Ferneley's family – John, Sally, Mary, William, Claud standing, Reuben sitting on a cushion. Mrs Sally Ferneley faces her children.

A drawing by Charles Simpson of the famous rough-rider Dick Christian on Lord Grey. Dick was born in March 1779 at Cottesmore near Oakham and died in June 1862 aged 84, living most of his life in Melton Mowbray. He was considered to be the finest horseman in England in his time. Married three times, his first wife bore him twenty children, his second only one. He took part in many steeplechases riding against the nobility of the day on equal terms. An eyewitness to the Cribb–Molineux fight at Thistleton Gap, he stated years later that 'I could hear the blows as plain as a drum beat.' This was the first defence of the heavyweight boxing championship of the world, in which Tom Cribb was the winner after eight rounds, on 28 September 1811.

The artist Sir Francis Grant on Grindal, by John Ferneley. A self taught artist, Grant first exhibited at the Royal Academy in 1834 at the age of 31, sending 'The Melton Breakfast'. Page 18 in *Around Melton Mowbray in Old Photographs* illustrates the second version of this famous painting. In 1840 he showed a painting of Queen Victoria in Windsor Park in his Academy exhibition. He then became the painter of the day. Elected President of the Royal Academy in 1866, Grant was knighted by the Queen shortly afterwards.

Headstone of Sir Francis Grant's grave in St Mary's Close, off Norman Way. Sir Francis died suddenly in October 1878. His family and friends declined the honour of a burial at Westminster Abbey. Three hundred members of the Royal Academy joined the many hundreds who attended one of the most impressive funerals ever to be held in Melton Mowbray.

Sir Malcolm Sargent as a young man. He was organist and choirmaster at St Mary's church from 1914 to 1924. He is seen here in 1928.

Newsagent Mr E. Williams (height 47½ inches, weight 5 stone 6 pounds). He was a popular trader between the two world wars on the streets of Melton Mowbray.

Dick Burton VC unveiling the war memorial to the dead of the Second World War in the garden of remembrance at Egerton Lodge on 1 August 1948. Dick was educated at the Melton Modern Boys School on Limes Avenue, being awarded the VC in 1944 for action against the enemy 'way beyond the call of duty' during the Second World War.

The Countess of Wilton at a meet of the Belvoir Hunt in Egerton Park on 30 January 1914.

Senior Warden of the Town Estate in 1937, Mr S.B. Weaver.

Junior Warden of the Town Estate in 1937, Mr Len Leader.

Melton Urban District Council, 1937. Back row, left to right: C.S. Jenkins, J.G. Devitt, P.D. Prior, J. Litchfield, A.L. Sleath, H.K. Barker, W. Jarvis. Front row: T.R. Stockdale, F.R. Bailey, T. Brown, W. Greaves, H. Richardson, G.W. Selby, O. Brotherhood, S. Weaver.

Leicestershire County Council area surveyor, 1937, Captain F.C. Salmon.

Melton Urban District Council treasurer, 1937, Mr C.S. Jenkins.

Sanitary inspector for the Rural District Council, 1937, Mr A.L. Sleath.

Area surveyor for the Rural District Council, 1937, Mr L. Hesford.

Melton Urban District Council, 1949–50. Back row, left to right: E.C. Moorhouse, C.S. Jenkins, H.K. Barker, F.J. Buckmaster, W.H. Jarvis, H. Buxton, J.W. Mills, G.P. Salt. Front row: J.W. Greenslade, Mrs A.G. Marsh, E.M. Summers, S. Berry, W. Greaves, E.B. Eagles.

Presentation by Councillor Frank Buckmaster of the chain of office of Melton Urban District Council to Stanley Berry JP, Chairman 1950–1, on 23 May 1951.

Photograph of staff and Councillors to the Melton Urban District Council in front of Egerton Lodge, 1973. From back row, left to right: Paul Raymond, Bill Forkes, Mike Missett, Ted Howarth, Roy Mound, Charles Bird, Jack Martin, Walter Marshall, Tony Emmerson, Wilf Taylor, Jim Beeson, Lee Jamieson, Bryce Gommersall, Charles Bird, Mike Robinson, Jim Boyland, Charles Townend, –?–, Jack Wildman, Lesley Leng, Herman Hinchcliffe, Ray Bailey, Mrs Basford, Jack Stevenson, Dorothy Maycock, Gill Cross, Ron White, Theresa Pytlik, John Spence, Janet Hall, –?–, –?–, –?–, Joan Turner, Edith Clarke, Angela Manning, Jane Watson, Terry Larder, Jenny Smith, Moira Hughes, Rita Borrow, Beck Simpson, Susan Gamble, Susan Poulson, Maisie King, Angela Fielding, Charlotte Needham. Councillors: –?–, –?–, Burton, Littlewood, Jane, Mrs Gell, Towel, Greenslade, Green, Salter, Sanders.

High jinks in Egerton Park at the Hospital Fête, June 1936. Daniel Hayes, fishmonger, of 33 Market Place is holding the donkey's head. Harold Pearce, gents outfitter, of 18 Market Place (Swan Porch) is behind the donkey organizing the rides, with Archie Sleath, sanitary inspector for the Rural District Council, cane at hand in case of trouble, on the extreme right of the photograph.

Leicestershire County Constabulary, Melton Mowbray Division, 1937. Back row, left to right: PCs Crowder, Smith, Pratt, Cliff, Humberston, Jasper, Webster. Middle row: PCs Goldstone, Blundy, Neale, Hewitt, Geary, Claxton, Baker, Jarvis, Topps, Bason. Front row: Sergeants Rickett, Meakin, Jones, Superintendent Gotheridge, Sergeants Hull, Bramall, Cave.

Melton Mowbray Fire Brigade, 1937. Back row, left to right: L. Haycox (inset), F. Stapleford, H. Beeken, F. Wood, G. Hack, C.E. Dawson, A.E. Rippon (inset). Front row: Capt F.G. Smith, H. Wallace, G.H. Newbold, D.A. Cunington.

Notable doctors in the town of Melton Mowbray during the 1930s and 1940s. Dr M. Dixon MD, BSc, Dr M.C. Elliott MB, Dr R.H. Fagge MRCS, Dr H.S. Furness MD.

Acknowledgements

The compilation of this book was only made possible by the help of many friends of the author. They have provided photographs and information without which this book could not have been published. Permission has been granted for all the photographs that are still in copyright. Should any person consider copyright material has been used without the holder's permission, the author offers his sincere apologies and will make an acknowledgement in future publications.

The basis of this collection of photographs is the author's own collection. The following people have provided help in many ways. The author's good friend Rigby Graham offered advice and provided the photographs of the goods yard in the town railway station, and excellent photographs recording the demolition of the Northern station. As usual, Nigel Moon gave good advice, and also provided the photograph of the bridge on Scalford Road and two other photographs. Margaret Portess provided many of the photographs and was able to assist in the compilation of many of the captions. Joe Ecob and Alan Richardson allowed the author access to their large collection of historic photographs; with their help the compilation of this book was made a lot easier.

Mr Peter Herrick, Borough Secretary and Clerk to the Melton Borough Council, gave the author permission to delve into the council archives; he was helped by Elaine Ferney, the tourism officer, and Marcia Coxhead. Many of the 'official' photographs came from this source. Bob Dove of the planning department provided the photograph of the crane on p. 89. Mrs S. Tindall provided the photographs on p. 131. Walter Robertson gave helpful advice on Royal families and provided the photographs on pp. 144 and 145. Jimmy Learmonth was extremely helpful as usual in providing information about and photographs of football teams in the Melton area. Ian Hickman provided a number of photographs covering cricket in the town. Gordon Williams, an 'Old Meltonian', was extremely helpful. He provided many photographs, but above all gave help and advice on compiling the captions.

Thanks are due to Mr and Mrs A. Charles for their professional help and for allowing the author permission to reproduce photographs from their collection. Christine Greaves, External Relations Administrator for Pedigree Petfoods, was most helpful and provided full permission to use photographs which are that company's copyright. No book of photographs depicting scenes of Melton Mowbray life would be complete without Stilton cheese and pork pies being included. The manufacturers of these products, Tuxford and Tebbutt, are part of the history of the town, and their factory manager, Mr A.M. Farquharson, provided an excellent collection of photographs for the author's use, without any restrictions being applied. Thanks are also due to the author's wife Pamela for tolerating a husband whose collecting habits tend to overshadow their household at times. Finally, thanks are due to Pat Peters for neatly typing the text for the publisher's use.